The Art of COOKING FOR SINGLES

By Jim Ressis

Based on
Healthy Recipes and Tasty Food

ISBN 0-9650456-0-9

Printed in Canada

INTRODUCTION

In 1980 I found myself living alone and in need of nutritious, delicious food which I had become accustomed to over the years. My employment at the time did not allow me to spend much time in the kitchen preparing meals. I found, however, that I had plenty of time during the weekends to keep a house and do my cooking. I decided to pre-cook most of my meals for the week, divide them into individual servings, freeze them, and reheat them as I needed. I came up with a number of recipes that would maintain their flavor and texture over a period of being frozen and then thawed. Every morning before I left for work I would remove an individual serving and place it in the refrigerator. In the evening I would quickly microwave or reheat it in a few minutes.

I treated several of my single friends and some of my dates to my special meals and discovered, to my surprise, that my cooking was a hit. They could not tell that the meal was prepared well in advance. When my guests realized what I was doing, they demanded copies of my recipes.

As a native of Athens, Greece I grew up watching my mother prepare family meals using techniques passed down over the centuries. I gradually became aware of the delicate blance of herbs and spices. When I found myself having to prepare my own food, I drew from my experience of seeing my mother cook. I remembered that her leftovers always tasted better the second day, and I assumed that flavors enhanced when the food is left for a period of time.

Living and working in the United States, I had to modify those recipes to become more suitable to western tastes and to the health-conscious consumer of today. My recipes are based on foodstuff readily available at your corner grocery store, and I have religiously avoided the use of saturated fats, replacing them with more healthy and tasty olive oil.

My spices are also commonly found in most kitchens, and I never use specialized utensils. The recipes are easy to follow. I believe that most single people of today, with busy schedules and a demanding lifestyle, would be happy to be able to prepare simple, delicious, nutritious dishes designed for the single person, or create a feast of several courses for their guests.

As a longtime member of single clubs and gourmet groups, I continuously surprise them with meals based on my own recipes. The demand for my recipes among my single friends has been so great that I decided to put everything I know in the form of a book with the hope that it may prove useful to single people of all ages.

This book also includes appetizers for a cozy evening or a party of several guests.

In addition, this book includes the nutritive value of foods and other hints and suggestions for preparing meals.

Jim Ressis
Rochester, New York

PREFACE

As a member of a prominent and well established "Gourmet" singles dinner club, of which Jim is a fellow member, I have been privileged to sample a wide selection of the delicious dishes that Jim delights in preparing for the whole group. His recipes, many of which are original to Jim, are always looked forward to with anticipation and received with great favor by everyone.

Having had the opportunity of reviewing many of Jim's personal recipes, it is obvious that their wonderfully appetizing and nutritional nature will endear them to all those who enjoy good food, especially to single people everywhere.

One of the outstanding features of this book is the simplicity of Jim's recipes, which generally require only ingredients found in the average kitchen, making it extremely easy for even the most novice cook to follow the simple directions and enjoy the rewards of "gourmet" cooking.

John Simon

Rochester, New York

TABLE OF CONTENTS

SOUPS

PORK

PASTA

SAUCES

FISH

PARTY MEATBALLS

1-1½ lbs. ground beef
1 egg, beaten
1 medium size onion, grated
2 tablespoons olive oil
2 tablespoons parsley, chopped
1 teaspoon mint, chopped
1 cup bread crumbs
½ teaspoon oregano
salt and pepper to taste
flour
oil for frying

1. Sauté onions until soft in 2 tablespoons oil in a small frypan.

2. Beat egg lightly in a medium size bowl. Add ground beef, breadcrumbs and mix by hand.

3. Add remaining ingredients except flour and oil. Mix well by hand. With moistened hands shape into small balls about ¾" around.

4. Roll in flour and fry in hot oil until brown all sides.

Variation:
Use the same recipe for larger meatballs for spaghetti sauce (meatballs 1½" around).

SPINACH TRIANGLES

1 lb. spinach
½ lb. feta cheese
4 tablespoons butter, melted
1 large onion, chopped
1 teaspoon dill, chopped
1 egg, beaten
2 tablespoon olive oil
½ cup bread crumbs
2 tablespoons grated cheese
salt and pepper

1. Wash spinach, discard stems, and cut spinach into small pieces.

2. Sauté onions in oil until soft.

3. Place spinach in a colander to drain and rinse with cold water. Place spinach into a medium size bowl and add the onions with the oil and mix well by hand.

4. Crumble feta cheese into small pieces.

5. Add feta into the bowl with grated cheese, beaten egg, salt and pepper, bread crumbs, dill; mix well.

6. Remove phyllo dough from the package.

7. Unfold 4 sheets on flat surface and cut phyllo into 4" x 12" strips (reroll remaining phyllo in wax paper).

SPINACH TRIANGLES CONTINUED:

8. Taking one sheet at a time, brush with melted margarine.

9. Fold sheet in half lengthwise and brush again with melted margarine.

10. Place 1 teaspoon spinach mixture in one corner of the strip and fold into triangular as you fold a flag.

11. Arrange on baking sheet and brush the tops with melted butter and bake at 375° until golden brown and crisp (about 15 minutes).

12. Allow to cool before serving.

SPINACH ROLLS

1. Same recipe as spinach triangles (see page 8).

2. Cut phyllo into 4" x 12 " strips.

3. Place on sheet, short side in front of you, and brush top with melted butter.

4. Drop 1 teaspoon spinach mixture into the center 1" from the end nearest you.

5. Fold the leaf from the right side , toward the center, covering the mixture (filling). Do the same from the left side.

6. Now roll away from you and place in buttered baking sheet. Bake at 375° for 15 minutes until golden brown and crisp.

EGGPLANT DIP

1 large eggplant
1 clove garlic, crushed
1 lemon, juiced
salt and pepper
½ cup olive oil
2 tablespoons parsley, finely chopped
3 tablespoons soft breadcrumbs

1. Bake eggplant on baking tray about 30-40 minutes until skin is soft.

2. Let cool for 3 minutes. Cut in half.

3. Using a spoon, remove seeds and scoop out eggplant. Place into a blender with lemon juice. Blend at medium speed, gradually adding olive oil and mixing well until smooth and thick.

3. Add crushed garlic, parsley, breadcrumbs, and salt and pepper to taste. Continue mixing until it becomes a smooth paste.

4. Place into a dish. Serve with crackers or bread.

FISH ROE DIP (Greek Tarama)

2 tablespoons tarama
1 small onion, finely chopped
1 cup olive oil
3 slices white bread
½ lemon, juiced

1. Place finely chopped onions, tarama, and a little oil in a mixing bowl and mix well.

2. Moisten bread, remove crust, and squeeze out excess water.

3. Place bread into mixer, add lemon juice and olive oil gradually. Increase speed of mixer and mix until fluffy.

4. Transfer to a dish. Serve with bread or crackers.

CHICKEN LIVER

1 lb. chicken liver
2 tablespoons olive oil
1 teaspoon dried oregano
½ cup sweet red wine
salt and pepper to taste

1. Trim fat from the liver and sprinkle with salt and pepper.

2. In a frypan, heat oil and sauté the liver, stirring occasionally to sauté all sides.

3. Add the oregano and wine.

4. Cover and cook for ten minutes.

Serve as appetizer.

SWEET AND SOUR MEATBALLS

1½-2 pounds ground beef
3 slices white bread
1 small onion, finely chopped
1 egg
1 tablespoon vinegar
½ cup white sugar
2 tablespoons flour
2 cups water
2½ tablespoons soy sauce
salt and pepper to taste

1. Mix ground beef, onion, salt, pepper, bread, and egg.

2. Form into meatballs and sauté in frypan. Turn occasionally to brown on all sides.

3. Prepare sauce by mixing sugar, vinegar, flour, water, and soy sauce; pour over meat balls.

4. Transfer to a baking dish and bake at 350° for 30 minutes.

Serve over rice, macaroni, or with baked potato.

OVEN POT ROAST

Small bottom round beef
2 tablespoons olive oil
1 large onion, sliced
3 medium carrots, diced
4 medium stalks celery, diced
4 potatoes, quartered
3 cups cold water
salt and pepper to taste

Place the meat in a roasting pan. Brown meat in a preheated oven at 400° for 15 minutes. Occasionally turn meat to brown all sides. Remove from the oven and add all the ingredients. Cover with foil and bake at 350° for 1½-2 hours until meat is tender.

BEEF ROAST

2-3 lb. beef roast, rump or chuck

1. Wash meat with cold water. Place beef roast in a roasting pan.

2. Rub meat with salt and pepper to taste and place in a preheated 400° oven and bake for ½ hour.

3. Add 1 cup of cold water and 1 tablespoon margarine.

4. Reduce heat to 350° and cook for 2 hours; baste and turn occasionally.

5. Let cool for 10-14 minutes before carving.

Serving size approximately ½″ slice.

BEEF POT ROAST

2-3 lb. pot roast
2 tablespoons flour
3 tablespoons margarine
½ cup sweet red wine
2 large onions, sliced
1 can tomato sauce (14½ oz.)
2 cups water
2 large carrots
3 celery stalks, halved
3 large potatoes
salt and pepper to taste

1. Season meat with salt and pepper and rub in the flour.

2. In a saucepan, melt the margarine and brown the meat on all sides.

3. Add the tomato sauce and remaining ingredients. Bring to boil, cover and simmer for 2½-3 hours.

BEEF PATTIES (Broiled)

1 lb. ground beef
1 small onion, finely chopped
1 slice fresh white bread, remove crust
1 egg
½ tablespoon olive oil
½ teaspoon oregano
salt and pepper to taste

1. Combine all ingredients in a bowl and mix.

2. Shape the patties into about 4 oz. portions (¾" x 3"thick). Broil the patties under moderate heat until done.

FRIED BEEF LIVER

Use baby beef liver.

baby beef liver (1 thin slice per person)
1 medium onion, rings
3 slices of bacon
2 tablespoons flour
2 tablespoons olive oil
salt and pepper to taste

1. In a hot frypan add two tablespoons olive oil and sauté onion until soft. Remove onions from the frypan.

2. Place flour into a dish and rub the liver with the flour.

3. In the same frypan, fry liver until cooked (not too dry).

4. Add onion and bacon and fry until bacon is done. Stir occasionally.

Serve with baked or fried potatoes.

BEEF STEW

1½-2 lbs.	beef stew
1	large onion
3	medium size potatoes, peeled and cut into quarters
2	carrots, cut in small pieces
2	celery stalks
1	bay leaf
1	can stewed tomatoes (14.5 oz.)
1	tablespoon flour
1	package stew mix
	salt and pepper to taste

1. Cut beef stew in half (1" cubes) and trim the fat.

2. Heat 2 tablespoons oil in 4 qt. saucepan and brown meat all sides (about 10 min.).

3. Remove the meat from the pan and set aside. In the same saucepan sauté onion. Discard oil.

4. Place meat into 6 qt. stockpot. Add the onion, potatoes, celery, bay leaf, stewed tomatoes, 4 cups water, 2 tablespoons olive oil and flour. Stir all ingredients. Bring to boil. Add the stew mix and stir well. Reduce heat, simmer 1-1½ hours.

Variations:

1) Potatoes, corn, peas, string beans.
2) Brown meat. Place in a crockpot with other ingredients and cook overnight on low heat. *Note: Do not freeze potatoes.*

BAKED MEAT LOAF

2-3 lbs. lean ground beef
1 medium size onion, diced
1 cup seasoned bread crumbs
1 egg, beaten slightly
1 tablespoon olive oil
1 cup tomato sauce
salt and pepper to taste

1. In a large bowl mix the ground beef and all the ingredients. Form the mixture into a Pyrex loaf pan or a baking pan.

2. Pour the tomato sauce on top of the meat loaf.

3. Bake at 350° for 1½ hours. Let cool for 5 minutes and cut the loaf into 1" slices.

Serve with rice, egg noodles, or mashed potatoes.

CUBED STEAKS SAUTEED WITH ONIONS AND MUSHROOMS

2 cube steaks
1 large onion, sliced
1 small can mushrooms, chopped
2 teaspoons margarine
½ cup sweet wine
salt and pepper to taste

1. Place cube steaks into a large frypan and sauté cube steaks for about 5 minutes.

2. Drain all the fat and add 2 teaspoons margarine.

3. Place into the chopped onions and mushrooms in the frypan and season with salt and pepper.

4. Sauté all together for 15 minutes. Turn occasionally.

5. Add ½ cup dry or sweet wine and cook until done.

Serve with microwaved potatoes.

Microwaved Potatoes: Slice microwaved potatoes and garnish with the onion and mushroom mixture on top of the potatoes. Place one cube steak next to potato on each dish.

CHILI WITH GROUND BEEF

1 large can red kidney beans
1 large can whole tomatoes
½ cup celery
1 teaspoon chili powder
1½ lb. ground beef
¼ teaspoon sugar
salt and pepper to taste

1. Sauté ground beef for 5 minutes and discard grease.

2. Place ground beef into saucepan and add tomatoes, onion, salt, pepper, chili powder, celery, sugar, and beans.

3. Cook over medium heat for about 1½-2 hours.

Flavor improves if allowed to stand overnight or for a few days and then reheated.

Serve with fresh bread and a tossed salad.

STUFFING FOR CHICKEN OR TURKEY

1. Sauté onions and celery in butter or oil until tender but not browned.

2. Cut bread into small pieces (½" x ½" inch).

3. Mix bread and vegetables in a medium size baking pan or 2 qt. covered casserole.

4. Add the herbs, salt and pepper and mix lightly until all ingredients are well mixed. Add chicken broth little at the time and mix.

   Stuff chicken or turkey loosely.

Variation I:
Use sausage, chestnuts, mushrooms or giblets.

Variation II:
Use oven cooking bag to bake chicken or turkey. Cook in plastic bag, everything cooks up tender, juicy and there's no messy pan or oven to clean.

GRILLED CHICKEN

Use chicken breast or quarters.

3 tablespoons olive oil
2 tablespoons dried oregano
½ teaspoon pepper
1 lemon, juiced
½ teaspoon salt

1. In a saucepan, boil chicken for 15 minutes.

2. In a bowl, prepare the mixture of olive oil, salt, pepper, oregano, and juice of 1 lemon; stir well.

3. Place foil on the grill and place chicken on the foil. Baste with the olive oil mixture. After 5 minutes turn chicken and baste with the mixture. Occasionally turn and baste chicken until fully cooked. Remove chicken when cooked.

ROAST CHICKEN WITH POTATOES

2-3½	lbs. chicken
2	lemons, juiced
1	tablespoon dried oregano
½	teaspoon thyme
2	tablespoons margarine
2 lbs.	potatoes, peeled and quartered
2	cups cold water
	salt and pepper

1. Remove giblets from the chicken and wash chicken with cold water. Place chicken in a roasting pan and bake 30 minutes in a 400° oven.

2. In a mixing bowl, place the peeled and quartered potatoes, juice of two lemons, and salt and pepper. Toss potatoes by hand to mix with the lemon.

3. Remove chicken from the oven and arrange the potatoes around chicken and add 2 cups of cold water. Return roasting pan to the oven. Bake for 1½-2 hours. Turn and baste the potatoes occasionally.

BAKED CHICKEN WITH LEMON

2-3 lbs. chicken
1 lemon, juiced
¼ stick margarine
2 cups cold water
1 tablespoon olive oil
salt and pepper to taste

1. Remove giblets from the cavity and wash chicken with cold water. Rub chicken with olive oil and salt and pepper.

2. Preheat oven to 450°. Place chicken in a roasting pan. Add water, the juice from the lemon, and margarine.

3. Place roasting pan in the oven and bake chicken for 30 minutes. Turn heat down to 350°. Occasionally baste with the fat in the roasting pan (every 10 min.) and finish baking. Total baking time 1½ hours. Use the fat to make gravy and pour over the chicken.

Gravy: Place the fat from the roasting pan in a saucepan and on low heat on the stove, add 2 tablespoons flour and stir until smooth.

Serve over rice, macaroni, or egg noodles

DEEP FRIED CHICKEN

Use drumsticks, thighs, or chicken breast.

Note: See Deep Fried Fish.

Variation:

For large quantity, place chicken on well greased aluminum foil on baking sheet. Bake for 45 minutes at 350°. As one side is browned turn the pieces over. Serve with fried or baked potatoes.

ROAST CHICKEN WITH BARBECUE SAUCE

3-3½ lbs. chicken
2 cups hot water
salt and pepper to taste
oil
paprika
barbecue sauce

1. Remove plastic bag with giblets from the chicken and wash chicken with cold water.

2. Rub the skin with oil and season the inside of the chicken with salt and pepper and the outside with paprika. Place chicken on roast rack in a roasting pan with 2 cups hot water.

3. Place the chicken in preheated oven at 400°. After 10 minutes turn oven down to 325°.

4. When the chicken has been in the oven about 30 minutes, brush the chicken with barbecue sauce on all sides and turn the chicken breast side up. For the entire cooking baste the chicken with the drippings in the roasting pan. Cooking time about 1½ hours.

Use the drippings in the pan for gravy. Serve with rice pilaf, macaroni, or french fries.

CHICKEN WITH TOMATO SAUCE

2 pieces chicken, thighs or breast:

1. Brown chicken all sides in 2 tablespoons butter. Season with salt and pepper on all sides.

2. Cook covered over low heat for 15 minutes.

3. Make tomato sauce (see Tomato Sauce recipe,)
4. Place cooked chicken in the tomato sauce and simmer for 15 minutes.

5. Serve over rice, macaroni, or spaghetti with a salad.

BROILED MARINATED CHICKEN BREASTS

2 boneless skinless broiler-fryer chicken breast halves
1 clove garlic, minced
½ teaspoon chopped basil
½ teaspoon thyme
¼ teaspoon pepper
¼ cup wine vinegar
¼ cup orange juice
salt to taste

1. Sprinkle chicken on both sides with garlic, basil, thyme and pepper; arrange chicken in shallow bowl.

2. Mix together vinegar and orange juice and pour over chicken. Cover and refrigerate for at least 2 hours.

3. Place chicken on boiler pan. Set temperature control at broil 500°. Arrange oven rack so chicken is about 4″ from heat. Broil, turning, about 6 minutes per side or until fork can be inserted in chicken with ease.

4. Sprinkle with salt and serve with wild rice, pouring pan drippings over rice.

Makes 2 servings.

ELEGANT GARLIC CHICKEN FOR TWO

2 broiler-fryer chicken quarters
2 tablespoons margarine
1 clove garlic, minced
1 medium onion, sliced
2 cloves
1 bay leaf, broken in half
½ teaspoon salt
½ teaspoon coarsely ground pepper
1 cup white wine
½ cup sour cream

1. In medium frypan, place margarine and garlic over medium heat, about 2 minutes or until garlic is light brown.

2. Add chicken and cook, turning, about 10 minutes or until brown on all sides.

3. Place onion slices on bottom of pan under chicken; add cloves and bay leaf.

4. Sprinkle chicken with salt and pepper; pour wine over chicken. Cover, reduce temperature to low and simmer about 40 minutes or until fork can be inserted into chicken with ease.

5. Remove chicken to serving plates and keep warm.

6. To pan drippings, add sour cream and cook, stirring, about 2 minutes until warm but not boiling. Spoon over chicken.

CHUTNEY CHICKEN AND RICE FOR TWO

1 cup cooked, diced broiler-fryer chicken
¼ cup peach preserves
¼ cup pineapple preserves
2 tablespoons chicken broth
1 tablespoon prepared mustard
1 tablespoon red wine vinegar
1 tablespoon chopped raisins
1½ teaspoon minced onion
½ teaspoon curry powder
½ teaspoon ground ginger
2 cups cooked rice
½ cup unsalted dry roasted peanuts

1. In a small frypan, over medium heat, place peach preserves, chicken broth, mustard, vinegar, raisins, onion, curry powder, and ginger.

2. Stir and heat until hot, about 4 minutes. Stir in diced chicken and rice and heat until warm, about 3 minutes.

3. Reduce temperature to low and let cook about 5 minutes more to blend flavors.

4. Sprinkle with peanuts.

Makes 2 servings.

HOT GREEK CHICKEN SALAD

8 broiler-fryer thighs, skinned
¼ cup cornstarch
3 tablespoons olive oil, divided
2 cups cauliflowerets
½ pound fresh whole green beans, trimmed
2 small zucchini, thinly sliced
1 garlic clove, crushed
1 can (8 oz.) tomato sauce
2 tablespoons water
½ teaspoon garlic salt
½ teaspoon dried oregano leaves, crushed
½ teaspoon dried rosemary leaves, crushed
2 small tomatoes, quartered
½ cup pitted Greek black olives, sliced
8 crisp lettuce leaves
1 cup feta cheese, crumbled

1. Cut chicken from bone into ½″ cubes.

2. In shallow dish, place cornstarch. Add cubed chicken and roll to coat.

3. In a large frypan, place 2 tablespoons oil and heat to medium-high temperature. Add chicken and stir fry about 4 minutes or until firm and lightly browned; remove chicken from frypan and set aside.

4. Add remaining 1 tablespoon oil to frypan and heat to high temperature.

HOT GREEK CHICKEN SALAD CONTINUED

5. Add cauliflower, green beans, zucchini and garlic; stir fry about 2 minutes or until vegetables are crisp-tender.

6. Return chicken to frypan. Add tomato sauce, water, garlic salt, oregano, and rosemary. Reduce heat to low temperature, cover and simmer 5 minutes.

7. Stir in tomato and olives.

8. Arrange lettuce on serving dish. Spoon chicken mixture over lettuce. Sprinkle with feta cheese.

Makes 8 servings.

VEGETABLE CHICKEN CURRY

8 broiler-fryer chicken thighs, boned and skinned
2 tablespoons margarine
2 tablespoons olive oil
1 large onion, thinly sliced
2 garlic cloves, minced
1 tablespoon curry powder
½ teaspoon coriander seed, crushed
½ cup water
3 cups red potatoes, unpeeled and cubed
2 cups carrots, sliced
2 cups mushrooms, quartered
1 cup frozen peas, thawed
1 cup plain yogurt

1. In a frypan, place margarine and olive oil and heat over medium heat until margarine melts. Add onion and garlic; saute about 7 minutes or until onion is soft.

2. Stir in curry powder and crushed coriander seed.

3. Add chicken, turning to coat.

4. Add water, potatoes, carrots, and mushrooms. Cover and simmer over low heat, about 25 minutes or until vegetables are tender crisp and fork can be inserted in chicken with ease.

5. Add peas and steam until hot; stir in yogurt.

PARTY CHICKEN (Small Bites)

1 small chicken or chicken parts
1 cup barbecue sauce
2 tablespoons olive oil
1 lemon, juiced
salt and pepper to taste

1. Wash chicken with cold water. Place chicken or parts in a roasting pan skin side down.

2. Bake chicken in 400° oven for ½ hour. Remove pan from the oven and let cool for 15 minutes. Drain the fat from pan.

3. Cut the wings from the breast and cut the thighs. Cut the breast or thighs in thin slices and into small pieces. Place pieces in a roasting pan.

4. Sprinkle with salt, pepper, juice of 1 lemon and barbecue sauce. Mix very well.

5. Bake at 350° for 45 minutes. Stir occasionally.

Serve over pilaf or as an appetizer.

Chicken pieces could be used in place of whole chicken.

ROAST LEG OF LAMB WITH LEMON

2-3 lbs. leg of lamb
2 cloves garlic
2 lemon, juiced
2 teaspoons margarine
salt and pepper to taste

1. Wash leg of lamb with cold water. Rub with salt and pepper.

2. Cut two slits over surface of the leg and insert the garlic into the slits.

3. Place in a preheated 400° oven. Roast lamb for ½ hour, turning occasionally to brown both sides.

4. Lower heat to 350° and pour the lemon juice on top of the lamb.

5. Place the margarine on the lamb and add 2 cups of cold water.

6. Bake for 2½ hours or until done.

7. Let cool for 15 minutes. Slice about ½″ thick portions.

Serve with pasta or rice.

ROAST LEG OF LAMB WITH LEMON CONTINUED

Variation I:

Potatoes, peeled and quartered, may be cooked with lamb.

Variation II:

3-4 lbs.	potatoes, peeled and quartered
3	cups hot water
1	lemon, juiced
½	teaspoon dried oregano
2	teaspoons margarine
	salt and pepper to taste

1. Roast lamb in a 400° oven for ½ hour.

2. In a mixing bowl place peeled and quartered potatoes. Add the lemon juice, salt, pepper, and oregano. Toss potatoes by hand to mix with lemon. Place potatoes around lamb and add three cups hot water.

3. Add margarine on top the potatoes and return roasting pan to the oven.

4. Bake for 2½ hours or until done, turn and baste the potatoes and lamb occasionally. When done remove lamb.

5. Increase oven to 400° and brown potatoes about 20-25 minutes longer.

BAKED LAMB WITH PASTA

leg of lamb
1 can tomato sauce 14.5 oz.
5 cups hot water
½ lb. orzo pasta or macaroni
2 tablespoons grated cheese
1 clove garlic
salt and pepper to taste

1. Roast lamb (see Leg of Lamb).

2. Slice meat into small slices.

3. Add hot water into the roasting pan, pasta, margarine, and tomato sauce.

3. Reduce oven temperature to 350° and bake until pasta is cookked.

4. Stir occasionally.

5. Bake for about 1½-2 hours or until pasta is done.

6. Remove from heat and let stand covered for 15 minutes.

Serve with grated cheese.

LAMB CHOPS

lamb chops (1 per person)
1 tablespoon margarine
½ lemon, juiced
½ tablespoon dry oregano
salt and pepper to taste

1. In a hot frypan, heat margarine.

2. Sprinkle chops with salt, pepper, and oregano.

3. Place chops in the frypan and cook both sides until done. Turn occasionally.

4. Remove from the frypan and sprinkle with lemon juice before serving.

Serve with pilaf or bake potato.

Variations: Use beef steaks, rib eye, T-bone, porterhouse.

LOW-CAL SALAD DRESSING

1 cup tomato juice
½ lemon juice of
1 teaspoon onion, chopped
1 teaspoon celery, finely chopped
1 teaspoon green pepper, finely chopped
salt and pepper to taste

Place in a jar and shake well.

TOMATO SALAD (Greek Salad)

1. Wash tomato and cut into small, uniform pieces. Peel and cut onion into thin slices; separate into rings. Dice green onion.

2. Sprinkle the salad with salt and oregano; toss lightly.

3. Add feta cheese.

Serve with olive oil and vinegar dressing.

POTATO SALAD

2 medium size potatoes, peeled
1 small onion, sliced
½ teaspoon olive oil
½ teaspoon vinegar
1 teaspoon fresh parsley, chopped
½ teaspoon oregano
salt and pepper to taste

1. Peel potatoes and cook in boiling, salted water until tender. Drain and cool for 2 minutes.

2. Slice the potatoes into a bowl.

3. Add sliced onion (rings), salt, pepper, oregano, parsley, oil, and vinegar.

4. Toss lightly.

Serve chilled.

VEGETABLE SALAD

1 can green beans, drained
1 can yellow beans, drained
1 can kidney beans, drained
1 tablespoon olive oil
2 tablespoons red wine vinegar
salt and pepper to taste

Mix all ingredients together in a large bowl and let stand for ½ hour.

CHICKEN EGG-LEMON SOUP

Chicken Soup:

2-3 lb. stewing chicken (half chicken)
½ teaspoon salt
½ cup rice

1. Wash chicken with cold water and place in large kettle with boiling water.

2. Cook for 1-1½ hours until tender. Add salt during the last ½ hour of cooking.(Remove scum)

3. Remove chicken and the fat. Add the rice and cook until tender.

4. Remove from the heat and wait for the boiling to stop. Add Egg-Lemon Sauce below.

5. Cut chicken into small bite-size pieces and place in the soup.

6. Remove soup from heat.

Variations:

1) Add carrots, onions, and celery stalk.
2) See Chicken with Tomato Sauce.

EGG-LEMON SAUCE

2 egg whites
1½ lemons, juiced

1. Beat egg whites well and gradually add the lemon juice.

2. Add hot liquit from chicken slowly to egg whites beating constantly.

3. Return to heat and stir until thickened.

BEEF BONE SOUP WITH PASTA

1 beef soup bone
1 large onion
1 cup chopped celery
1 tablespoon olive oil
1 small can diced tomatoes or tomato sauce
carrots, celery, onion, chopped
⅓ cup orzo or barley
salt and pepper to taste

1. Rinse bone with cold water to remove blood and impurities. Place bone in pot and cover with water. Bring to boil, reduce heat and simmer, removing the scum. Boil for about 2 hours. Remove beef bone.

2. Add remaining ingredients to the liquid. Cut meat into small pieces and place into the soup. Simmer about ½ hour.

BEAN SOUP

1 can white kidney beans
1 tablespoon olive oil
1 small onion, chopped
1 small can tomato sauce
½ cup chopped celery with leaves
1 small carrot diced
salt and pepper to taste

Combine the beans in a small kettle with olive oil, tomato sauce, onion, celery, carrot, salt and pepper. Cook for ½ hour.

FRENCH ONION SOUP

1½ tablespoons butter
3 large onions, sliced
5 cups or 2 cans beef or chicken stock
pepper
French bread (2 slices)
Swiss cheese

1. Heat the butter in small kettle. Add onions and cook until golden (do not brown onion). Add stock and bring to boil for 15 minutes.

2. Pour soup into soup bowls.

3. Season to taste. Cut bread ½ " thick slices (1 slice per bowl of soup) and toast. Place the slice of bread on top of the soup and cover with cheese.

4. Bake in preheated oven at 350° until the cheese is bubbling.

Variation:
1 can chicken broth and 1 large onion makes 1 bowl.

TOMATO AND LENTIL SOUP (For Two)

3 oz. lentils
1 small carrot, diced
1 small onion, finely chopped
½ cup celery, finely chopped
1½ tablespoon olive oil
8 oz. tomatoes, diced
1 teaspoon tomato paste
½ teaspoon sugar
3 cups water or stock
1 bay leaf
1 clove garlic, chopped
1 tablespoon vinegar, wine, or tarragon
salt and pepper

1. Wash the lentils. Place in saucepan (2 qt.), heat olive oil and sauté onion, garlic, carrots, celery, and lentils for 10 minutes.

2. Add tomatoes, tomato paste, water or stock, seasonings and bring to a boil. In the last 15 minutes of cooking add salt to taste.

3. Stir in vinegar before serving.

TOMATO SOUP:

1 can diced tomatoes
1 carrot, diced
½ cup celery, diced
2 cups water
1 tablespoon olive oil
½ teaspoon sugar
1 tablespoon parsley
salt and pepper to taste

1. Sauté onion in olive oil until tender.

2. Add tomatoes and continue to sauté for about 3 minutes.

3. Add water, salt, celery, carrots, parsley, sugar and pepper. Bring to a boil and simmer for 15 minutes.

Variation:
Add ½ cup barley.

MACARONI SOUP

1 can beef broth
1 cup macaroni
salt and pepper to taste

1. Boil water with salt and add macaroni to boiling water. Cook for 10 minutes.

2. Drain and add beef broth.

3. Bring to a boil and season with pepper.

4. Cook for 15 minutes.

TURKEY SOUP

1. Break turkey carcass into pieces and remove all stuffing.

2. Place carcass in large soup pot along with some pieces of meat. Cover with water and bring to boil. Boil for about 1 hour.

3. Strain the liquid into an other pot and remove bones and fat.

4. Add salt and pepper to taste, 1 cup chopped celery, 1 cup chopped carrots, and 2 large potatoes peeled and quartered.

5. Cover and simmer about 1½ hours.

ROAST PORK

Pork loins or center cut
½ cup onions, chopped
½ cup celery, chopped
½ teaspoon sage
1 tablespoon olive oil
salt and pepper to taste

1. Sauté onions in olive oil in a frying pan, turning occasionally until soft (about 5 minutes).

2. Add celery and sauté for 2 minutes.

3. Wash pork with cold water. Sprinkle with sage, and salt and pepper to taste.

4. Place pork into a roasting pan, fat side up. Preheat over to 450°. Roast uncovered for ½ hour.

5. Turn oven temperature down to 350°. Remove roast from oven and place onions and celery in the bottom of the pan. Continue roasting until done.

Total cooking time is about 2-2½ hours. Turn and baste occasionally during the roasting period.

PORK CHOPS WITH APPLES

Pork chops
Apples
Margarine (1 teaspoon)
Salt and pepper to taste

1. Wash pork chops and sprinkle with salt and pepper to taste.

2. Melt margarine in frying pan. Add pork chops and cook on high heat until brown and tender.

3. Slice apples about ½" thick. Fry in the remaining drippings in the pan.

BARBECUED SPARERIBS

4-5 lbs. beef or pork spareribs
salt and pepper to taste
1 cup barbecue sauce

1. Wash spareribs with cold water. Rub with salt and pepper and place on the grill.

2. Brush them with barbecue sauce. Cook one side for 5 minutes; turn them over and brush other side with barbecue sauce. Turn occasionally.

3. Cook until done. About 45 minutes.

SWEET AND SOUR SPARERIBS

3 lbs. spareribs
1 tablespoon olive oil
1 medium size onion, chopped
½ cup water
¼ cup ketchup
¼ cup brown sugar
1 tablespoon vinegar
2 tablespoons soy sauce
salt and pepper to taste

1. In a frypan, brown spareribs with the onions.

2. Add the water, salt, and pepper; cover and simmer for about 45 minutes.

3. Mix brown sugar, ketchup, and vinegar; simmer for 10 minutes. Add soy sauce and pour the mixture over the spareribs.

4. Simmer for 30 minutes.

STUFFED PORK CHOPS

See turkey stuffing.

1. Cut chops along the side to make pocket.

2. Fill with stuffing and fasten with toothpicks to close.

3. Place into a baking pan and bake for 1 hour.

Variation:

Pour tomato juice around chops and slice tomato on the top.

GREEK BAKED MACARONI (PASTICHIO)

1 lb. long ziti (thick pasta)

See Greek Meat Sauce

See Cream Sauce

1. In a large pot, cook ziti in boiling, salted water until just tender.
2. Drain ziti and place a layer in a deep baking pan. Sprinkle with grated cheese.
3. Add a layer of meat sauce and one more layer of ziti sprinkled with cheese.
4. Cover ziti with cream sauce and bake at 350° for 45 minutes or until cream sauce turns light brown.

GREEK MEAT SAUCE (Spaghetti Sauce)

1-1½ lbs.	ground beef (90% fat free)
1	medium onion, diced
1	16 oz. can diced tomatoes
1 ½	tablespoon olive oil
1	tablespoon parsley
½	teaspoon oregano
1	cinnamon stick
1	garlic clove, minced
½	teaspoon sugar
	salt and pepper to taste

1. Place ground beef in a small kettle with 1 cup of water and simmer for 5 minutes, stirring occasionally, until light brown. Drain all liquid.

2. In a large frypan heat oil and sauté onions for 2 minutes; add garlic and sauté both until onions are soft.

3. Increase heat and add ground beef and remaining ingredients.

4. Cover and simmer for 30 minutes.

5. Remove cinnamon stick before serving.

Serve on top of spaghetti, egg noodles, or any other pasta, and with grated cheese.

BROWN SAUCE

1 tablespoon margarine
1 carrot, thinly sliced
1 onion, sliced
1 bay leaf
1 tablespoon parsley
4 tablespoons flour
1 14 oz. can beef broth
½ teaspoon thyme
salt and pepper to taste

1. Melt margarine in a saucepan and sauté onion, carrot, bay leaf, thyme, and parsley until brown.

2. Add the flour, stirring constantly until well browned.

3. Add beef broth and bring to a boil for about 15 minutes.

4. Strain and add the salt and pepper.

Variation:
Add small can mushrooms well drained, rinse and cut in slices. Sauté mushrooms with the onions.

CREAM SAUCE

1 tablespoon butter or margarine
½ cup flour
2 cups milk
½ teaspoon nutmeg
1 egg, lightly beaten
salt and white pepper

1. Melt margarine in a saucepan.

2. Add milk and bring to a boil (for 1 minute); stirring constantly.

3. Add flour and stir until smooth. Add nutmeg and salt and pepper to taste.

4. Remove from heat and let cool a little before stirring in the egg.

THIN WHITE SAUCE

1 tablespoon margarine
2 tablespoons flour
1½ cups milk (2%)
½ teaspoon salt
white pepper to taste

1. Melt margarine in a saucepan.

2. Add flour and stir thoroughly, then pour in the milk while stirring constantly.

3. Bring to a boil (for 3 minutes). Remove from heat.

ITALIAN MEAT SAUCE

1-1½ lbs. stewed meat
1 small hot Italian sausage, (½-1½ lbs.)
1 16 oz. can stewed tomatoes
1 16 oz. can tomato sauce
1 medium onion, grated
2 cloves garlic, minced
1 tablespoon parsley, chopped
1 teaspoon dried or fresh basil leaves
½ teaspoon oregano
2 tablespoons tomato paste
2 tablespoons olive oil
½ teaspoon sugar
2 cups water
salt and pepper to taste

Heat the oil in a saucepan until very hot. Add the stewed meat and brown well on all sides. Add the onions and garlic to the pan and sauté until golden and soft. Brown sausage in a small frypan until brown on all sides; cut sausage into small bite size pieces and add into pan with meat. Add tomatoes and all remaining ingredients and simmer for ½-1 hour. The longer you simmer, the tomato sauce develops a mellow flavor.

Serve as topping on spaghetti or macaroni with grated cheese.

MEAT SAUCE

1-1½ lbs. ground beef
1 medium size onion, chopped
1 can (16 oz.) tomatoes, diced or stewed
½ teaspoon sugar
2 tablespoons olive oil
1 tablespoon chopped parsley
½ teaspoon oregano
1 clove garlic, chopped
½ stick cinnamon
1½ cups water

1. Cook ground beef with 1 cup of water over low heat for 5 minutes, stirring occasionally until ground beef begins to brown. Drain well in a colander.

2. Sauté onions and garlic in olive oil until golden and soft. Add ground beef, other ingredients and seasonings. Cover and simmer over gentle heat for 15 minutes.

3. Remove cinnamon stick before serving.

Serve over spaghetti or macaroni.

Cooking spaghetti: cook in boiling, salted water until tender. Drain and return to pan on low heat. Add 1 tablespoon butter and stir into spaghetti. Serve with grated cheese and top with meat sauce.

PLAIN TOMATO SAUCE

1 large can stewed tomato or crushed tomatoes
2 tablespoons olive oil
1 large onion, finely chopped
1 clove garlic, finely minced
1 teaspoon dried oregano
2 tablespoons dried parsley or fresh, chopped
1 stick cinnamon
½ teaspoon sugar

1. In a large fry pan heat 1 tablespoon olive oil and sauté onions until soft.

2. Add tomatoes and all ingredients and simmer over low heat for about 20 minutes or until sauce is stiff enough but not too dry.

3. Remove cinnamon stick before serving.

Serve as topping on spaghetti, macaroni, rice, poultry. Use the same tomato sauce for baking fish with tomato.

TOMATO SAUCE

1 can diced or stewed tomatoes (16 oz.)
1½ tablespoon olive oil
1 medium size onion, chopped
1 tablespoon parsley
½ teaspoon oregano
1 clove garlic, crushed or ½ teaspoon powder
½ stick cinnamon
½ teaspoon sugar
salt and pepper

1. Heat oil and fry onion until light golden and soft.

2. Add all ingredients; cover and simmer for 15 minutes.

Serve over spaghetti, rice pilaf, or egg noodles.

TOMATO SAUCE WITH FRESH TOMATOES

1. Peel tomatoes and cut into thick slices.

2. Place tomatoes in a pan and simmer until soft.

3. Rub tomatoes through a sieve.

4. In a hot saucepan sauté onion. After two minutes add 1 teaspoon garlic (chopped) and simmer till onions are soft.

5. Add tomatoes, salt and pepper to taste and continue cooking, stirring constantly.

6. Add ½ teaspoon sugar, ½ teaspoon dried oregano, and 1 small cinnamon stick.

7. Cook for ½ hour.

Serve with spaghetti.

Variation: Add a small can mushrooms well drained, rinsed, and sliced. Sauté mushrooms with onion and garlic.

MARINATING OR BARBECUE SAUCE

1½ cups lemon juice
½ cup olive oil or vegetable oil
1 clove garlic, crushed
1 teaspoon oregano
salt and pepper

1. Combine all ingredients. Pour over meat or chicken and mix well.

2. Refrigerate overnight. Use the sauce on meat or chicken while grilling or broiling.

<u>MAYONNAISE</u> (Homemade)

2 eggs
3-4 teaspoons mustard
½ teaspoon sugar
½ teaspoon salt
white pepper
2½ tablespoons lemon juice
½ cup olive oil

Using a small mixing bowl and spoon, or small mixing bowl and electric mixer; stir egg yolks with mustard, sugar, salt and pepper until smooth. Very slowly, add olive oil alternately with the lemon juice and continue mixing until thick.

NOTE: Beating the egg yolks well in a bowl is important for good emulsion. Should mayonnaise break, it can be rescued.

Beat an egg yolk in a bowl and very slowly begin again to beat the broken mayonnaise.

OCTOPUS WITH TOMATO SAUCE AND RED WINE

1-2 lbs. cleaned octopus
2 onions, finely chopped
2 tablespoons olive oil
1 can (16 oz.) stewed tomatoes
1 bay leaf
¾ cup sweet red wine or cream sherry
1 clove garlic, crushed
salt and pepper

1. Place cleaned octopus in heavy pan with 1 cup water. Cover and simmer for 20 minutes.

2. Remove octopus from heat and rinse with cold water.

3. Sauté onions in oil until golden and soft.

4. Cut octopus into bite-size pieces and place in a pan. Add onions with oil, tomatoes, bay leaf, garlic, salt and pepper, and water to cover.

5. Bring to a boil and simmer for 1 hour.

6. Add wine and simmer for another ½ hour, or until octopus is tender.

Serve as an appetizer or as topping on spaghetti or macaroni.

FRIED SQUID

4 squid, cleaned (dinner for two):
salt
lemon
flour
oil

1. Use ready cleaned squid. Slice in ½" rings or strips and sprinkle with salt.

2. Coat squid with flour and fry in shallow frypan for 5 minutes, a few pieces at a time. Turn over until evenly browned.

3. Serve with lemon juice.

Fried squid makes a good appetizer.

BAKED FISH

2 pieces of Cod fillets or 1 large piece (about 12 oz.)
1 lemon, juiced
2 tablespoons butter or olive oil
1 can diced tomatoes (optional)
1 large onion, sliced
2 cloves garlic, crushed
⅓ cup parsley, chopped
½ cup dry wine

1. Brush fish with lemon juice and butter or oil and place in 350° oven and cook about 15 - 20 minutes.
2. Sauté onion until golden and soft.
3. Pour over the fish. Add tomatoes and the remaining ingredients and cook covered for 20 minutes.

4. Halfway through the cooking time check the fish. If it appears to be drying out, spoon some of the sauce over the fish.

5. Garnish with lemon slices and parsley.

Variations:
Substitute other fish; Snapper, Bass (fillets), Flounder, Bluefish, *whole Bluefish.

DEEP FRIED FISH

Haddock (fillets)
Bass (fillets)
Smelts
Flounder (fillets)
Blue fish (Fillets or steak)

4 oz. flour
1 whole egg
1 cup milk
½ cup bread crumbs
salt and pepper

1. Wash and scale the fish. Place flour in a dish.

2. In a shallow bowl beat the egg with milk.

3. Place bread crumbs in another dish. Season fish with salt and pepper.

4. Bread fish with flour and beaten egg; press firmly in the bread crumbs.

5. Fry in hot oil or butter until golden brown.

6. Drain and serve, garnished with parsley and lemon and with tartar sauce.

Fried breaded shrimp: peel, devein, butterfly, and fry as above.

TARTAR SAUCE

1 small dill pickle
1 teaspoon capers
1 medium size onion
3 tablespoon mayonnaise
½ tablespoon parsley, chopped

1. Cut pickles and onions into small pieces and place in a small stainless mixing bowl. Add capers and mix well.

2. Drain all liquid. Add all ingredients and mix.

MASHED POTATO PUFFS

5 medium size potatoes
1 egg yolk, well beaten
½ cup grated cheese
2 tablespoons hot milk
1 teaspoon dried parsley
1 small onion, finely grated
1 tablespoon soft margarine
¼ teaspoon paprika

1. Scrub potatoes and boil them in salted water until soft. Peel boiled potatoes under running cold water and mash.

2. Add hot milk, cheese, egg yolk and mix until fluffy.

3. Season mixture with parsley, paprika, onion, salt, and pepper.

4. Place mixture in refrigerator to cool (about 20 minutes).

5. Melt margarine.

6. In a greased pan, place two tablespoons of mixture for each pancake. Brush tops with the melted margarine.

7. Bake puffs about 20 minutes in preheated 350° oven. Turn them occasionally to brown both sides.

Serve them plain or with syrup.

STUFFED TOMATOES WITH MEAT SAUCE AND RICE

8 firm tomatoes
See Greek Meat Sauce

1. Wash tomatoes with cold water. Cut through the top of the tomatoes (thin slice).

2. Scoop out tomato pulp and discard all seeds and chop pulp; put aside.

3. Prepare meat sauce; add two extra cups of water.

4. Bring to a boil and add one cup rice. Stir to mix with the meat sauce and cook about 10 minutes. Remove from heat.

5. Place tomatoes in baking pan. Sprinkle inside of tomatoes with salt to taste. Fill tomatoes with meat and rice mixture.

6. Rub tomato pulp through a sieve and pour the juice on tomatoes.

7. Pour some tomato juice around the tomatoes and pour olive oil on top (about 3 tablespoons); sprinkle with small amount of breadcrumbs.

8. Add 1 cup of water to the baking pan and bake at 350° for 45 minutes or until cooked; baste with the liquid from the pan.

OKRA WITH TOMATO SAUCE

1 lb.	fresh okra
1	small onion, sliced
2	tablespoons olive oil
1	cup tomato sauce or diced tomatoes
1½	cup cold water
2	medium size potatoes, thinly sliced (¼" thick)
	salt and pepper to taste

1. Wash fresh okra and remove the cone-shaped top.

2. In a hot frypan heat 1 tablespoon olive oil and sauté okra for 10 minutes. Occasionally turn okra to sauté all sides. Remove okra from the frypan.

3. In the same frypan add 1 tablespoon olive oil and sauté onions until golden and soft.

4. In a saucepan, place the sliced potatoes, okra, onions, water, and tomato sauce.

5. Add salt and pepper to taste.

6. Cook for 30 minutes.

GREEK MOUSSAKA (EGGPLANT DISH)

1 medium-size eggplant
3 medium-size potatoes

1. Slice eggplant and place in a colander and sprinkle with salt. Let stand in the colander for 30 minutes to drain.

2. Peel potatoes and slice 1/4" thick. Sprinkle with salt.

3. Overlap a layer of potatoes in a greased 10" x 16" x 2" pan.

4. Overlap a layer of eggplant on top of the potatoes.

5. Cover eggplant with meat sauce (see Meat Sauce).

6. Cover with Cream Sauce and bake in a 350° oven for 1 hour or until golden brown.

See Cream Sauce

FRIED VEGETABLES

Carrot sticks
Celery
Broccoli
Cauliflower
Green pepper
Onion
Zucchini
Mushrooms
2 tablespoons olive oil

Batter

1 cup flour
1¼ cup water
1 egg, well beaten
salt and pepper to taste

1. Mix batter until well blended; chill.

2. In frypan, heat oil. Coat vegetables with batter and fry until golden brown.

3. Serve with rice and tomato sauce.

DILL PICKLES

10 small pickling cucumbers
3 cups white vinegar
½ cup pickling spice
1 garlic clove
1 teaspoon dill seeds or fresh dill
pickling salt

1. Wash cucumbers with cold water and place them in a bowl. Cover them with pickling salt for 24 hours.

2. Place cucumbers in a ceramic bowl. Mix vinegar with salt and pour over the cucumbers. Add pickling spice and dill. Add more water, if needed.

3. Place a dish on top to hold them down in brine. After 3 days seal them in a sterilized jar.

PICKLED ONIONS

1 lb. frozen small onions
3 cups white vinegar
2 tablespoons salt
2 tablespoons pickling spice.

1. Place onions in a bowl and cover them with water and add the salt. Let stand for 48 hours.

2. In a saucepan, bring vinegar to a boil. Add onions and boil them for 3 minutes.

3. Place onions and pickling spice in sterilized jar. After a week they will be ready.

PICKLED VEGETABLES

Cauliflower, pieces
Green beans
Small onions, peeled
Small pickling cucumbers
Carrots, sticks

1. Wash cauliflower and separate into florets leaving portion of stalk attached. Sprinkle with salt and let stand for 24 hours.

2. Clean beans and onions, and cut beans, onions, cucumbers, and carrots into small pieces.

3. Boil water with two tablespoons of salt and drop in the beans, onions, cucumbers, cauliflower, and carrots; boil for 1 minute.

4. Place vegetables and pickling spice in a jar and cover with boiling vinegar. Let cool. Seal jar.

FRUIT SALAD

1 cup pineapple tidbits, drained
1 can fruit cocktail (about 14-oz.), drained
1 small can tangerine segments, drained
1 cup miniature marshmallows
1 egg
½ cup light cream
1 tablespoon sugar
1 lemon, juiced
1 cup whipped cream

1. Place all fruit in a bowl and add marshmallows.

2. Beat the eggs until light and gradually add sugar, light cream, and lemon juice.

3. In a double boiler, cook until thick, stirring constantly.

4. Cool and add whipped cream.

5. Pour into the fruit mixture and mix.

6. Chill for 24 hours.

Serve as dessert.

BAKED APPLE

4 Servings

1. Cut out the core from each apple without cutting through to the bottom.

2. Stick a fork through the apple skin on top in 3 or 4 places.

3. Put apples in a small baking dish.

4. Mix sugar and cinnamon. Put 1 tablespoon of mixture into center of each apple.

5. Pour water around, not over, the apples. Cover dish.

6. Bake at 350° for about 1 hour or until apples are tender.

Other Filling Ideas:

Crushed pineapple packed in juice.
Raisins, alone or with sugar and cinnamon.

PINEAPPLE SWEET POTATOES

4 servings

½ tablespoon margarine
8 oz. can crushed pineapple in natural juice
2 cups sweet potatoes, fresh, cooked, and sliced
¼ teaspoon cinnamon
⅛ teaspoon salt

1. Heat margarine in a large frying pan.

2. Add sweet potato slices and pineapple.

3. Sprinkle with cinnamon and salt.

4. Simmer without a cover until most of the juice has cooked away. This may take 10-15 minutes.

5. Turn potato slices to coat them with the pineapple juice, then serve.

FRUIT MILK SHAKE

4 servings

3 cups fresh fruit in season, or canned fruit in light syrup or natural juice
½ cup nonfat dry milk powder
1 cup water or drained juice from can
8 ice cubes, crushed

1. Peel fresh fruit or drained canned fruit, preserving the liquid.

2. Cut fruit into pieces and mash through a strainer or with a fork.

3. Crush ice cubes by putting the cubes in a dish towel or heavy plastic bag. Crush them with a rolling pin or hammer.

4. Blend together fruit, nonfat dry milk powder, and water or drained juice. Add crushed ice and blend again.

VEAL CUTLETS

Veal slices from leg (½" thick)
3 tablespoons flour
1 egg well beaten
1 cup breadcrumbs
salt and pepper to taste

1. Wash veal with cold water.

2. Sprinkle with salt and pepper to taste.

3. Place the flour, egg, and breadcrumbs together in a dish.

4. Roll veal in the mixture. Fry slowly until well browned.

Variation: Place the cooked cutlets in a baking pan and pour meat sauce over top. Bake at 350° for 25 minutes. Serve with spaghetti or baked potato.

VEAL CHOPS

1 large veal chop or veal shoulder
2 tablespoons margarine
salt and pepper to taste
juice of ½ lemon
½ teaspoon dried oregano

1. Wash veal with cold water.

2. In a large frying pan, melt 2 teaspoons of margarine. Saute the veal (about 10 minutes on each side).

3. Add lemon juice, oregano, and salt and pepper to taste. Cover and simmer for about 5 minutes or until done.

4. Pour drippings over veal, and serve with rice pilaf or baked potato.

BASIC CHICKEN COOKERY

Chicken is one of the most adaptable of all foods. It can be prepared in literally hundreds of different ways, however, there are basic cooking methods which every cook should master.

Chicken prepared in any of the following ways is delicious served "as is" or it can be the basis of numerous creative chicken dishes. One 3½ lb. broiler-fryer chicken usually makes 4 servings.

ROASTER CHICKEN: Mix together 1 teaspoon salt and ¼ teaspoon pepper; sprinkle over outside of whole broiler-fryer chicken and inside body cavity. Hook wing tips under back of chicken. In shallow pan place chicken, breast side up. Roast in 350° oven for 1 hour or until internal temperature of 180° is reached. Let stand 10 minutes before carving.

FRIED CHICKEN: In plastic bag, mix together 1½ cup flour, 1 teaspoon salt, and ¼ teaspoon pepper. Add 1 broiler-fryer, cut-up chicken, a few pieces at a time, and shake to coat. In large frypan place ⅓ cup cooking oil and heat to high temperature. Add chicken, skin down; cook, uncovered, about 10 minutes, turning to brown all sides. Reduce heat to medium-low, cover and cook about 20 minutes more or until chicken is brown and fork tender. Drain on paper towels.

OVEN FRIED CHICKEN: In small frypan, melt ¼ cup margarine over medium heat. Remove from heat and stir in 1 teaspoon salt and ¼ teaspoon pepper. In shallow dish, place ½ cup dry breadcrumbs. Using 1 broiler-fryer, cut-up chicken, dip each part, one at a time, first in margarine and then in breadcrumbs, turning to coat well. On lightly greased baking sheet place chicken, skin side up, in single layer. Bake in 350° oven about 50 minutes or until chicken is brown and fork-tender.

SIMMERED CHICKEN: In deep saucepan, place 1 whole broiler-fryer chicken or 1 cut-up broiler-fryer chicken. Add 2 cups water, 1 teaspoon salt and ¼ teaspoon pepper (1 small onion, sliced and 3 celery tops may also be added if desired). Cover and simmer about 45 minutes or until chicken is fork-tender. Remove chicken from pan and cook; reserve broth for later use. Separate meat from bones; discard skin and bones. Cut chicken into bite-size pieces. Yield: about 3 cups diced, cooked chicken and 2-2½ cups broth.

GRILLED CHICKEN: On prepared grill with rack about 8 inches from heat source, place broiler-fryer chicken halves, quarters, or parts. Grill, turning frequently (using tongs to prevent piercing skin), about 1-1¼ hours or until fork-tender. Homemade or bottled barbecue sauce may be brushed on chicken during last 15 minutes of grilling time.

MICROWAVE CHICKEN: In shallow microwave dish arrange 1 cut-up broiler-fryer chicken (skin removed) in single layer with meatier parts toward outside of dish. Brush chicken with 1 tablespoon melted margarine. Cover with wax paper and microwave on HIGH 18-20 minutes (about 6 minutes per pound), rotating dish one-half turn after 9 minutes. Sprinkle with ½ teaspoon seasoned salt and let stand, covered, 5 minutes. Note: When microwaving whole bird, use MEDIUM temperature setting.

Whatever method you use for cooking chicken, the most accurate test for doneness is a meat thermometer. Whole chicken should reach an internal temperature of 180°. Bone-in part should reach a temperature of 170° and boneless parts should be cooked to a temperature of 160°. All juice should be clear, not pink, when chicken is pierced with fork.

Normally, chicken is done when a fork can be inserted with ease. Or, when cooking a whole bird, the leg should move freely when lifted or twisted. In microwaving, it is better to undercook than to overcook. Return to the microwave for 1 or 2 additional minutes if needed after checking for doneness.

Source: National chicken cooking contest

FOOD SOURCES OF ADDITIONAL NUTRIENTS

VITAMINS

Vitamin B_6

Bananas
Fish (most)
Liver & kidney
Meat
Poultry
Potatoes & sweet potatoes
Whole-grain cereals
Yeast

Vitamin B_{12}

(present in foods of animal origin only)
Cheese
Fish
Liver & kidney
Meat
Milk
Shellfish
Whole egg & egg yolk

Vitamin D

Egg yolk
Liver
Saltwater fish
Vitamin D milk

Vitamin E

Margarine
Nuts
Peanuts & peanut butter
Vegetable oils
Whole-grain cereals

Folacin

Dark green vegetables
Dry beans & peas
Liver
Wheat germ
Yeast

MINERALS

Iodine

Iodized salt
Seafood

Magnesium

Bananas
Cocoa
Dark green vegetables (most)
Dry beans & peas
Milk
Nuts
Whole grain cereals

Zinc

Cocoa
Dry beans & peas
Meat
Poultry
Shellfish
Whole grain cereals

Retail Cut and Method of Cooking

Chops or steaks for broiling or frying:

With bone and relatively large amount of fat, such as pork or lambs chops; beef rib, sirloin, or porterhouse steaks.

Without bone and with very little fat, such as round of beef, veal steaks.

Ground meat for broiling or frying, such as beef, lamb, or pork patties.

Roast for oven cooking (no liquid added):

With bone and relatively large amount of fat, such as beef rib, loin, chuck; lamb shoulder, leg; pork, fresh or cured.

Without bone.

Cuts for pot roasting, simmering, braising, stewing:

With bone and relatively large amount of fat, such as beef chuck, pork shoulder.

Without bone and with relatively small amount of fat, such as trimmed beef, veal.

COUNTS AS 1 SERVING

Breads, Cereals, Rice, and Pasta

1 slice of bread
½ cup of cooked cereal, rice, or pasta
1 oz. of dry cereal

Fruits

1 medium whole fruit
¾ cup of juice
½ cup of canned fruit

Dairy

1 cup of milk
8 oz. of yogurt
1 1/2-2 ounces of cheese

Meat, Poultry, Fish, Dry beans, Eggs, and Nuts

3 oz. of cooked meat, poultry, or fish
1/2 cup of cooked beans
2 tablespoons of peanut butter
1 egg counts the same as 1 oz. of meat

Fats, Oils, and Sweets
Use sparingly

How Many Servings Do You Need Each Day?

	Women, Some Teen Girls, Older Adults	Children, Boys, Active Women, Most Men	Teens & Active Men
Bread group	6	9	11
Vegetable group	3	4	5
Fruit group	2	3	4
Milk group	*2-3	*2-3	*2-3
Meat group	2	2	3

*Women who are pregnant or breastfeeding, teenagers, and young adults to age 24 need 3 servings.

The small tip of the Pyramid shows fats, oils, and sweets. These are foods such as salad dressings, cream, butter, margarine, sugars, soft drinks, and candies. Go easy on these foods because they have a lot of calories from fat and sugars, but few nutrients.

Did you know that being overweight can increase your risk of heart disease, diabetes, and some cancers? If you need to lose weight, you may need to eat less, exercise more, or do both.

Some foods are higher in calories than other foods. For example, foods that have more fat and sugar have more calories. Alcohol in beer, wine, and liquor also has calories. The way a food is made can also make a big difference in the number of calories. See the foods listed below.

Eating smaller servings of food will help you lose weight. A smaller serving has fewer calories than a large serving.

Be sure to exercise! Daily exercise can help you firm up your muscles, use up extra calories, and lose weight and keep it off.

If you eat less and exercise more, you can lose weight.

Here are some ways you can increase your daily exercise:

* Use the stairs instead of the elevator.
* Take a walk each day at lunch time or walk to work.
* Join an exercise class.
  (Check with your doctor before starting an exercise program)

This chart shows you how many calories you can use by doing 15 minutes of exercise. Compare that to just sitting. (see chart on the next page)

Activity (15 minutes)	Calories Used
Sitting	20 - 25
Walking	60 - 75
Bicycling	90 - 115
Jogging	145 - 180
Swimming	145 - 180

Cholesterol

You may have heard about cholesterol. Cholesterol is a fat-like substance that is found in foods from animal sources, such as meat, poultry, fish, egg yolks, milk, and milk products.

Cholesterol is not found in fruits, vegetables, breads and cereals, nuts, seeds, or dry beans and peas.

Your body needs some cholesterol for good health, but it makes enough by itself. The foods you eat can also affect how much cholesterol is in your blood.

Saturated fat is a kind of fat found mainly in foods from animals. Eating too much saturated fat and cholesterol raises blood cholesterol levels in most people. High blood cholesterol levels can increase the risk of heart disease. It is a good idea to limit the amount of fat, saturated fat, and cholesterol you eat.

Sodium

Type of Food (mg.)

Bread (1 slice) 110 - 175
Vegetables, fresh or frozen (½ cup) 0 - 70
Vegetables, canned (½ cup) 30 - 365
Soup, canned (1 cup) 810 -1,100
Fruit, fresh, canned, or frozen (½ cup) 0 - 10
Salad dressing (1 tablespoon) 80 - 220
Frozen main dish (8 ounces) 600 - 1,600
Potato chips or salted nuts (1 ounce)1 20 - 135

Here are some easy ways to lower the sodium in your meals:

* Use less salt or even no salt while you are cooking.
* Put less salt on your food at the table.
* Eat more fresh or frozen fruits and vegetables. These foods are low in sodium.
* Use herbs and spices to add flavor to your meals.
* Sodium is found in most foods you eat and drink. Sodium is a part of salt. Sodium is also found in other substances in foods. Mostof the sodium in your diet comes from salt already in foods you buy and salt you add to food in cooking or at the table.
* Eating less salt and sodium may be better for your heart and your blood pressure.
* Foods that are often higher in salt include cured and processed meats, bologna, sausage, and ham, canned vegetables, and some cheeses. Sodium is also found in many seasonings like soy sauce, garlic salt, and onion salt.
* Many foods now contain less sodium. These foods will have labels that say "reduced sodium," "no-salt-added," or "low sodium." Be sure to read the label and remember to look for both sodium and salt!

Get The Facts About Sugar

Think about the foods you usually eat. Do they have a lot of sugar?

Many of us eat too much sugar. Foods that are high in added sugar such as candies, soft drinks, and cakes are high in calories. Eating a lot of sugary foods can contribute to tooth decay and may add unwanted weight.

Shopping Tips:

* Buy 100% fruit juice without added sugar.
* Buy cereals that are not already sweetened with sugar.
* Buy fresh fruits or fruits canned in juice. They are naturally sweet.

Food labels tell you a lot about what is inside a can or package.

Sugars are listed in the ingredient label. Look for white sugar, brown sugar, honey, molasses, corn syrup, and other syrups.

Enjoy Grain Products

Grain products are good for you. They have vitamins, minerals, and fiber. They are low in fat, but are filling, and there are many kinds to choose from.

Choose some whole-grain foods every day. Whole-grain breads have more fiber than white breads. There are many kinds of whole-grain foods. For example, try whole-wheat breads, bran flake cereals, oatmeal, brown rice, corn tortillas, or popcorn. Aren't starchy foods fattening? Many people think starchy foods such as breads, rice, and pasta are fattening. They are not. But what you add when you eat them can make them fattening! For example, butter or margarine, mayonnaise, cheese sauce, or gravy can make the starchy foods fattening by adding many extra calories.

What is the Food Guide Pyramid?

The Food Guide Pyramid is an outline of what to eat each day based on the Dietary Guidelines. It's not a rigid prescription but a general guide that lets you choose a healthful diet that's right for you.

The Pyramid calls for eating a variety of foods to get the nutrients you need and at the same time the right amount of calories to maintain healthy weight.

Use the Pyramid to help you eat batter every day, the Dietary Guidelines way. Start with plenty of breads, cereals, rice, pasta, vegetables, and fruits. Add 2-3 servings from the milk group and 2-3 servings from the meat group. Remember to go easy on fats, oils, and sweets, the foods in the small tip of the Pyramid.

Source U.S.D.A Home and Garden Bulletin Number 250

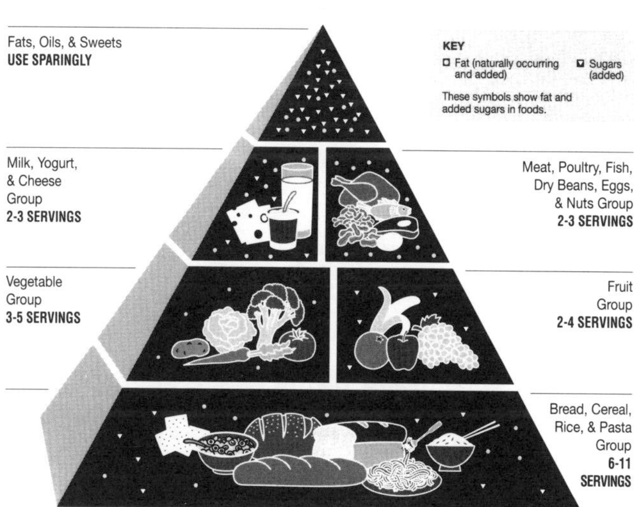

Here's a list of the spices you will need for most of the recipes in this book. As you can see, it's a lot less intimidating. Of course, you can substitute your own spices for some interesting results.

Black Pepper (ground)
Bay Leaves
Chili Powder
Cinnamon Sticks
Cloves
Curry Powder
Dill Seed
Dill Weef
Garlic Salt
Minced Onion
Mint
Mustard
Nutmeg (powder)
Oregano (dried)
Paprika
Pepper
Sage
Salt
Thyme
White pepper

Basic needs for your pantry:

1 can asparagus
1 can corn
1 can french type green beans
1 can mixed vegetables
1 can spinach
1 can tomato puree

1 can tomato stewed
1 can diced tomatoes
1 can zucchini
1 can green beans
1 can coffee, instant coffee & regular
1 box crackers
1 lemon
1 lime
1 can tomato juice
margarine
mayonnaise
beef steak
frozen fish
ground chuck
whole wheat bread
1 can mushrooms
Diet pop
eggs
chicken
frozen shrimp
liver
ground round
1 can tuna
non-dairy creamer
milk, skim
barbecue sauce
mild chunky salsa
salad dressing
broccoli
peas
potatoes
aluminum foil
cocktail sauce
rice

pork chops
pork roast
chicken breast
chicken quarters
freezer bags
vegetable oil

DO YOUR FRIEND A FAVOR...
IF YOU enjoy the
ART OF COOKING FOR SINGLES

it's likely your friends will enjoy it too. Print their names and addresses below, and we'll mail it to them in no time.

Please send me ______ copies.

TO ____________________

____

____

Book - $9.95
Postage and handling - $3.50

Number of books ________
Postage and handling ________
New York sales tax 8% ________
Total Enclosed $ ________

Make money order payable to:
Jim Ressis
P.O. Box 67549
Rochester, NY 14621

DO YOUR FRIEND A FAVOR...
IF YOU enjoy the
<u>ART OF COOKING FOR SINGLES</u>

it's likely your friends will enjoy it too. Print their names and addresses below, and we'll mail it to them in no time.

Please send me ______ copies.

TO ____________________

____

____

Book - $9.95
Postage and handling - $3.50

Number of books __________
Postage and handling __________
New York sales tax 8% __________
Total Enclosed $__________

Make money order payable to:
Jim Ressis
P.O. Box 67549
Rochester, NY 14621

DO YOUR FRIEND A FAVOR...
IF YOU enjoy the
ART OF COOKING FOR SINGLES

it's likely your friends will enjoy it too. Print their names and addresses below, and we'll mail it to them in no time.

Please send me ______ copies.

TO ______________________

____

____

Book - $9.95
Postage and handling - $3.50

Number of books __________
Postage and handling __________
New York sales tax 8% __________
Total Enclosed $__________

Make money order payable to:
Jim Ressis
P.O. Box 67549
Rochester, NY 14621